God's Bles.
Jack & Thelma Colman

Holle & Carol Plaehn
9/10/2005

Pastor Holle Plaehn

Plaehn Words from the Hill

Selected Sermons from 32 Years of Ministry to Peace Evangelical Lutheran Church and the Hilltop Community

By

Holle Plaehn

authorHOUSE™

1663 LIBERTY DRIVE, SUITE 200
BLOOMINGTON, INDIANA 47403
(800) 839-8640
WWW.AUTHORHOUSE.COM

First published by AuthorHouse 05/13/05

ISBN: 1-4208-1889-9 (e)
ISBN: 1-4208-1888-0 (sc)

Printed in the United States of America
Bloomington, Indiana

This book is printed on acid-free paper.

I give thanks for God's love in Jesus. I dedicate these sermons in honor of Carol – my wife, my friend, and my partner in the Gospel. I also dedicate these sermons in honor of my children – Kristin, Andrew, Gretchen, Janna, Micah, and Jon. Yes, and I want to thank Teryl Dirks, without whom this project would not have been possible or completed. Thanks be to God!

INTRODUCTION TO
"Plaehn Words from the Hill"

". . . This is what the Lord requires of you: to do what is right,

to love mercy,

and to live humbly with your God."

Micah 6:8

This verse describes the author of this book. Holle Plaehn served as pastor at Peace Lutheran Church in the Hilltop area of Tacoma, Washington, from 1971-2003. You will hear the Lord speaking to you through these twelve sermons which he chose to share. His ministry inspired us to focus on what he called "five gemstones:" God's *Grace*; *Faith*; reaching out to others in *Friendship* and *Evangelism*, and *Inclusion*.

"We are to empower people. All people in God's church are to share their gifts, to lead, and to speak out of their spirit-filled heart." (August 17, 2003)

How blessed we were to have God's good and faithful servants Holle and Carol Plaehn in our midst!

Many thanks to Teryl Dirks for so carefully transcribing these twelve sermons for us. They will remain a blessing to all.

In loving regard,

Sonja Yeager
April 5, 2004

All proceeds from this book will be dedicated to the Peace Community Center Scholarship Fund, in Pastor Plaehn's name.

_1_

THE GOOD NEWS OF CHRISTMAS
Christmas Eve Candlelight Service

Monday, December 24, 2001

Luke 2: 1-20

"In those days a decree went out from Emperor Augustus that all the world should be registered. ²This was the first registration and was taken while Quirinius was governor of Syria. ³All went to their own towns to be registered. ⁴Joseph also went from the town of Nazareth in Galilee to Judea, to the city of David called Bethlehem, because he was descended from the house and family of David. ⁵He went to be registered with Mary, to whom he was engaged and who was expecting a child. ⁶While they were there, the time came for her to deliver her child. ⁷And she gave birth to her firstborn son and wrapped him in bands of cloth,

1

and laid him in a manger, because there was no place for them in the inn.

[8] In that region there were shepherds living in the fields, keeping watch over their flock by night. [9]Then an angel of the Lord stood before them, and the glory of the Lord shone around them, and they were terrified. [10]But the angel said to them, 'Do not be afraid; for see—I am bringing you good news of great joy for all the people: [11]to you is born this day in the city of David a Savior, who is the Messiah, the Lord. [12]This will be a sign for you: you will find a child wrapped in bands of cloth and lying in a manger.' [13]And suddenly there was with the angel a multitude of the heavenly host, praising God and saying, [14]'Glory to God in the highest heaven, and on earth peace among those whom he favors!' [15]When the angels had left them and gone into heaven, the shepherds said to one another, 'Let us go now to Bethlehem and see this thing that has taken place, which the Lord has made known to us.' [16]So they went with haste and found Mary and Joseph and the child lying in the manger. [17]When they saw this, they made known what had been told them about this child; [18]and all who heard it were amazed at what the shepherds told them. [19]But Mary treasured all these words and pondered them in her heart. [20]The shepherds returned, glorifying and praising God for all they had heard and seen, as it had been told them."

My theme this evening is The Good News of Christmas.

Have you lost something because of September 11? Maybe the hole was there for a long time but September 11, 2001, seemed to exacerbate (intensify) that pain, that problem.

I want to proclaim a good news message to you tonight. There is the Good News of Christmas and this news speaks directly to the tragedy of September and to our loss and pain.

Ponder with me on this precious evening the reality of the Good News of Christmas.

First of all, the Good News of Christmas comes <u>through God's love in Jesus the Messiah</u>. We have laid out for us tonight this incredible love story for the world, for you and me.

God cares deeply for the world. The evidence in nature is all around. The trees, the mountains, the flowers in our sanctuary, the birds speak to us. Yes, and God has spoken through the prophets of long ago and now. God has spoken through the children of Israel. But in these last days, God speaks through the Messiah – Jesus.

The Gospel writer Luke shares this awesome story as it comes through the lives of ordinary, poor people. Luke shares their journey to Bethlehem, the tragedy of no place for them in the motel, Mary expecting with no family or friends but only the friendly beasts of the stable. The Child is born. No matter the opposition, God does come, for God has good news and that news must be delivered. God has devised a wonderful plan to win our hearts, to fill the hole in our lives. This Child is the fulfillment of the hopes and dreams of the children of Israel. God has now <u>sent</u> the promised Messiah. Christ has come. God has come to win our hearts with love.

The angels are singing outside Bethlehem to lowly shepherds. "Glory to God in the highest' and, yes, "peace," too. The angels proclaim, "Do not be afraid; for see, I am bringing you good news of great joy for all the people: To you is born this day in the city of David a Savior, who is the Messiah, the Lord."

Good news, friends. **The Good News of Christmas**.

Receive it.

Embrace it.

Receive God and God will do "God's thing" in your life.

The Good News of Christmas also comes to us <u>through God's love in others</u>.

There is even more good news tonight. I proclaim that God's love can be seen in 'other people' and that, too, is God's gift to you. These folks are everywhere – and they can and will help you.

Consider the examples of long ago:

- o Mary and Joseph

- o The saints of long ago

- o Famous saints like St. Francis, Martin Luther, Mother Theresa, and Dr. Martin Luther King, Jr.

Consider a few people who encouraged me recently.

- o A church in Parkland just called me up and said that they had gifts – lots of gifts – for needy families. What a joy to share!

- o Mrs. Martha Sarver – an old friend from Pennsylvania – taking care of her husband. This man had tutored me in ministry. Now he doesn't even remember me but she cares for this wonderful, jolly giant. Yes, and she sends me $1000 for our community center.

- o I think of the homeless man living in a van who stops by to give me $8 for the Peace Community Center – it is all he has!

- o I think of Ami, serving in Africa, who buys a turtle from a young lad trying to make some money for his family. He offers the turtle for half price – she paid him the full price.

- o I think of our precious youth and children sharing the Christmas program last week. What a gift to me – to us!

I could go on and on with these good news people and you have your own sets of examples, too.

There is Good News of Christmas <u>through God's love in you and me</u>! This incredible love is so contagious – so real – so life-giving that it is even possible for <u>you</u> and for <u>me</u> to be good news for our world.

God's love can make a decisive, deep impact so that we – you and I – can be good news. I spoke of the hole, the pain that can lead us to believe that we have little, even nothing, to share. The truth is that you have much to share. God has gifted you with talents, treasures, and time. God is with you in the Christ Child. God will help you share with your neighbors what they need.

I know most of you that are present this evening. I know you fairly well. (God knows you even better.) I know what you can do for others when God's love is at work in you. So I encourage you anew – even more important, the Christ Child encourages you anew – to continue, to become, to be God's good news to your world. In God, all things are possible.

I close with the poem, the prayer, of St. Francis*.

Lord, make us instruments of your peace.
Where there is hatred, let us sow love;
Where there is injury, pardon;
Where there is discord, union;
Where there is doubt, faith;
Where there is despair, hope;
Where there is darkness, light;

Where there is sadness, joy;

Grant that we may not so much seek to be consoled as to console; to be understood as to understand; to be loved as to love.

For it is in giving that we receive; it is in pardoning that we are pardoned; and it is in dying that we are born to eternal life. Amen.

*Lutheran Book of Worship

_2_

GOD'S STAR STILL SHINES
Epiphany Sunday

January 7, 1990

Matthew 2:1-12

In the time of King Herod, after Jesus was born in Bethlehem of Judea, wise men from the East came to Jerusalem, ²asking, 'Where is the child who has been born king of the Jews? For we observed his star at its rising, and have come to pay him homage.' ³ When King Herod heard this, he was frightened, and all Jerusalem with him; ⁴and calling together all the chief priests and scribes of the people, he inquired of them where the Messiah was to be born. ⁵They told him, 'In Bethlehem of Judea; for so it has been written by the prophet: ⁶"And you, Bethlehem, in the land of Judah, are by no means least among the rulers of Judah;

for from you shall come a ruler who is to shepherd my people Israel." ' ⁷Then Herod secretly called for the wise men and learned from them the exact time when the star had appeared. ⁸Then he sent them to Bethlehem, saying, 'Go and search diligently for the child; and when you have found him, bring me word so that I may also go and pay him homage.'

⁹ When they had heard the king, they set out; and there, ahead of them, went the star that they had seen at its rising, until it stopped over the place where the child was. ¹⁰When they saw that the star had stopped, they were overwhelmed with joy. ¹¹On entering the house, they saw the child with Mary his mother; and they knelt down and paid him homage. Then, opening their treasure chests, they offered him gifts of gold, frankincense, and myrrh. ¹²And having been warned in a dream not to return to Herod, they left for their own country by another road.

I declare to you today that **God's Star Still Shines**. I have reference to the star of Bethlehem. The one the wise men followed. No, not so much a physical star but a star that is just as real. Today we begin in the church the Epiphany Season. Epiphany, January 6, was once a major festival in the Christian Community. For the first three hundred years in church history, Epiphany was more prominent than Christmas. Epiphany means 'to reveal, to show, to expose'

– to be made manifest. The 'star' on our Christmas tree is an appropriate symbol for this season. A star brings light and this is the symbol I am using for this message.

Gracious Light

Rainbow Light

Reflected Light

Gracious Light

Long ago the wise men followed the star of Bethlehem and were led to the baby Jesus. The star was a gift from God that guided the wise men over a long, dangerous, and confusing journey. Without the star, the wise men would never have come into the presence of Jesus.

God provides a star for you and me. I should say stars – because there is more than one star for you and me. God guides us to the child through the gracious stars of the Bible, the church, spirit-filled people, our experiences, preachers – yes, even preachers! Are you aware of the gracious stars from God?

There is a caring man, a priest, who is a 'common sense' authority in chemical dependency issues. His name is Father Jack – he tells this story.

'Two hunters deep in the woods are huddled together around a camp fire. The conversation turns to religion. The first man speaks of his faith in God and how God has blessed him and guided him. The other man says, 'I don't believe in God. God has never helped me! In fact, I remember one time I specifically prayed to God. I was lost in the woods. I was desperate. Yes, I prayed but God doesn't care.' Both men were quiet for some time. Then the first man asked, 'But you are here, aren't you?' The second replied, 'Yes, I am here, but I would have died in the forest if that Indian guide had not come along to rescue me.'

Father Jack's point was that God uses a variety of ways (I call them gracious stars) to bless us – to guide us. The Bible, the church, spirit-filled people, and even preachers are some of the means to guide us on our journey of faith. In our journey, our gracious God guides us to Jesus. God desires to bring us to faith in Jesus – to trust Jesus!

Rainbow Light

The wise men were not Jews by nationality or race. They came from the East. The far East! They may have traveled for two years to reach Bethlehem. Who these mysterious folk were is a mystery, but the bottom line was not missed by early Christians. They saw in this story that God's gracious light is for all people. Jew and Gentile. Male and female. Slave and free. Rich and poor. I call this Rainbow Light – God's gracious Rainbow Light of inclusion. I am included – so are you.

This past Thursday I was walking the streets – talking to the young men and women selling drugs. I recall three young men. One seemed to stare into space as I talked with him. One asked for my prayers and volunteered his name. He wanted to make <u>sure</u> that I knew exactly for whom to pray. One wanted to talk but wasn't sure with his buddies around that he could converse with the preacher. In a sense, each person was confused and they probably didn't feel or believe that God included them in His gracious love.

How about you? Are you included by God? <u>God wants you</u>. You are significant – precious. Every person is precious – loved – the Child is for you. No matter your background. No matter your race. God sends light to guide you – to bring you to faith in Jesus.

Reflected Light

God's star still shines with gracious light – rainbow light – to <u>reflect</u> God's light from you to our world. Jesus said to his disciples, 'You are the light of the world.' (Matthew 5:14) Of ourselves, there isn't any light in us, but with God shining into our lives, we can be 'the light of the world.'

As the old Gospel song says,

> 'This little light of mine, I'm goin' a let it shine;
> This little light of mine, I'm goin' a let it shine;
> This little light of mine, I'm goin' a let it shine;

Let it shine, let it shine, let it shine.' (*This Far By Faith, Hymn 65*)

The wise men brought gifts. This is a new year. We/I/You can reflect the light of God. We can share what God has first given us. In the new year of 1990, we have light to reflect – God's light! Together as a community of faith we can bring light to the Hilltop Community and even for Tacoma.

Some people shine – their faith shines – the light of God is shining from them. This can be true for our church – for you and me. Not because we are so good but because God is able.

I want to close this message by asking you to consider gifts for the Christ Child even as the wise men brought gifts. I have six gifts that you may bring to the Child. These gifts are meant to be suggestive and to stimulate your life in Jesus.

1. Bring an open heart – be receptive to spiritual growth. Take time to read the Bible. Read the Bible 'through' in 1990!

2. Bring a witness for Jesus Christ. Share the Gospel. Invite family, friends, and neighbors to worship.

3. Bring a gift of peace to our world. Wherever – whomever – however that may be possible.

4. Bring a gift of justice. Focus on one of the big issues of our world. Mental Illness, World Hunger, Crime,

Racism, Violence, Addiction, Poverty. Take one of these – become more informed – act in some way – take a risk.

5. Bring a gift of personal life-style change. One step forward by God's help. Something jettisoned – something new – 'Spirit revealed' – but into that empty space!

6. Bring a gift to strengthen our church. Look around in the Spirit and see where you can make a difference in our community – the choir, tutoring, feeding program, breakfast program, usher – Whatever!

God's Star Still Shines.

Gracious Light

Rainbow Light

Reflected Light

_3_

CHRIST IS RISEN. HE IS RISEN INDEED!
The Festival of the Resurrection of Jesus the Christ

April 11, 1993

Matthew 28:1-10

After the Sabbath, as the first day of the week was dawning, Mary Magdalene and the other Mary went to see the tomb. ²And suddenly there was a great earthquake; for an angel of the Lord, descending from heaven, came and rolled back the stone and sat on it. ³His appearance was like lightning, and his clothing white as snow. ⁴For fear of him the guards shook and became like dead men. ⁵But the angel said to the women, 'Do not be afraid; I know that you are looking for Jesus who was crucified. ⁶He is not here; for he has been raised, as he said. Come, see the place where he lay. ⁷Then go quickly and tell his disciples, "He has been raised from the dead, and indeed he is going ahead of you to Galilee; there you will see him." This is my message for you.' ⁸*So they left the tomb quickly with fear and great joy, and ran to tell his disciples.* ⁹*Suddenly Jesus met them and said, 'Greetings!' And they came to him, took hold of his feet, and worshiped him.* ¹⁰*Then Jesus said to them, 'Do not be afraid; go and tell my brothers to go to Galilee; there they will see me.'*

There is the ancient greeting of Christians as they meet one another. One would declare "Christ Is Risen' whereupon the other believer would respond 'He is Risen Indeed!'

May we remember the purpose of this day as we follow their helpful greeting:

> Christ is Risen.
> He is Risen Indeed!
>
> Christ is Risen.
> He is Risen Indeed!
>
> Christ is Risen.
> He is Risen Indeed!

My, oh, my – what a great way to begin this message.

My friends, every August 10 at 3:30 p.m. Margaret and Erling Wold sit down and talk about an event that radically changed their lives twenty years ago. On that date, Pastor Wold was body surfing in the ocean near their home in Southern California. A huge wave caught Pastor Wold and dashed him to the beach, breaking his neck. He was now paralyzed from his head to his feet. Days later in the hospital he was informed that he would never walk again.

Ten years ago, I talked with Pastor Wold and his wife at Holden Village. He was walking and talking! God had performed a wondrous miracle. However, each year at 3:30 p.m., August 10, they gather to share and to remember. Margaret Wold said to me, 'On every anniversary of that ocean accident we talk about it, keeping the meaning of God's grace alive.'

The women go forth into the darkness in spite of the evil power of the Roman government who had crucified Jesus.

The women go forth in spite of the church leaders who would kill Jesus or anyone else in order to protect their own position and power.

The women went and may we give them much credit, but they sought a dead Jesus. They believed Jesus was dead and, friends, at times so do we! We, too, are convinced by our world that Jesus is dead. Our words and deeds betray Jesus and so we need to remember.

Remember the women.
Remember the earthquake.
Remember the stone was rolled away and the tomb was empty.

Remember the power of God for Jesus is not in the tomb.

Remember Christ is Risen. He is Risen Indeed!

Remember the words of the angel – 'Do not be afraid; I know that you are looking for Jesus who was crucified. He is not here; for He has been raised, as He said. Come, see the place where he lay.' (Matthew 28:6)

That became the marvelous, graceful news of the first Easter. The tomb is empty – Jesus is alive. Don't be afraid.

Jesus is alive – not because of our strength – rather because of the strong love of God.

Remember on that glorious morning the women are commissioned to be the first evangelists – 'Go and tell' the angel urges them. Go and tell the good news.

> Jesus is Risen.
> Jesus is Alive.
> Jesus will meet you.

As they go on the road, Jesus himself meets these ladies. There is an encounter with the living Lord Jesus. Wow, what a memory, what an anniversary we gather to remember.

This leads me to my second point – Response. What is my – your – response?

Have we gathered on this anniversary of the First Easter to talk about, to keep alive the memory of God's grace? Is my response <u>faith in Jesus</u>?

This past Thursday night I talked with Mai Shen – her husband, Pastor Joel Shen, had preached here last Sunday. Mai had a mastectomy recently. She reminded me that Friday would be <u>Good</u> Friday. Here is a lady my age, from China. She said, 'I am full of peace.' In spite of pain and sorrow she has responded in faith in Jesus. She spoke of her praying and caring friends. She was at peace.

Jesus is alive. Remember the first Easter. Jesus is here among us – with us. Jesus gives peace and hope no matter the circumstances.

Finally, I want to share that the first Easter is a time to remember, to respond with faith in Jesus, and a time for you and me to <u>go and tell</u>. Go and Tell!

The women at the tomb are the first evangelists – that is, 'good news' tellers of the Resurrection. Remember them. Remember that now is our time to go and tell. Go and tell that Jesus is alive. Go and tell in our words and deeds.

Long ago, there was once a mighty and generous Prince. His home was near a large city. Every morning he rode into the city on his beautiful horse. As he neared the city gates, there were many poor people gathered – waiting – hoping – looking for someone to help them in their misery. The Prince started a tradition of generosity. Every time he rode to the city, he would take out gold coins and give them to those in need.

One day, as he rode into the city, he remembered that he had not opened the gates of the stable for his horses. He feared for the horses' safety in the warm climate. He had a crucial meeting that now demanded his attention in the city. The Prince asked one of the men to whom he gave his coins if he or anyone of them would go for him to his home and tell the servants to open the stable gates. The Prince asked. He waited. He asked again and again! Silence. Finally, one man spoke in behalf of all. 'I will gladly take your alms (your gold coins) but I will not run your errands!'

God has been more than generous to us. God has given us more than silver and gold. Life. Hope. Jesus.

The question remains – will I do God's errands – will I go and tell?

I refer to a little lad of eight years who, with his sister of five years, has made a journey that leads to Easter. Austin goes to St. Francis Cabrini School in Lakewood, according to Kathleen Merryman in a recent article in the Tacoma newspaper. Austin has received a story from Matthew's Gospel that tells him to use his talents (gifts). Austin also has been given $6, as were other members of his class. Austin decides to help the homeless. He makes a list of what he wants to buy. His list is long – food, picture books, and Bibles.

He starts at Barnes and Noble – he explains his need to the clerk. She responds to him to put his money away. The store would not be able to donate but she would – she buys him $37 in books. Next store, a religious book store, the same thing happens. Next, he goes to Queen Anne Thriftway. He talks with the manager and once again he is told to fill up his shopping cart and everything is donated. The story ends with Austin going to his church where homeless families are living for the week. He brings his gifts and then he reads to the children in the shelter and makes new friends.

Austin said 'God has given me many gifts like a kind heart and a loving soul. I wanted to use those gifts to help others. I learned that when you do a kind act for others, it's contagious.'

Christ is Risen. He is Risen Indeed!

_4_

THE GREAT EVENTS NO ONE TALKS ABOUT
Ascension Sunday

May 22, 1977

Acts 1:1-11

'In the first book, Theophilus, I wrote about all that Jesus did and taught from the beginning ²*until the day when he was taken up to heaven, after giving instructions through the Holy Spirit to the apostles whom he had chosen.* ³*After his suffering he presented himself alive to them by many convincing proofs, appearing to them during forty days and speaking about the kingdom of God.* ⁴*While staying with them, he ordered them not to leave Jerusalem, but to wait there for the promise of the Father. 'This,' he said, 'is what you have heard from me;* ⁵*for John baptized with water, but you will be baptized with the Holy Spirit not many days from now.'*

⁶ So when they had come together, they asked him, 'Lord, is this the time when you will restore the kingdom to Israel?' ⁷He replied, 'It is not for you to know the times or periods that the Father has set by his own authority. ⁸But you will receive power when the Holy Spirit has come upon you; and you will be my witnesses in Jerusalem, in all Judea and Samaria, and to the ends of the earth.' ⁹When he had said this, as they were watching, he was lifted up, and a cloud took him out of their sight. ¹⁰While he was going and they were gazing up toward heaven, suddenly two men in white robes stood by them. ¹¹They said, 'Men of Galilee, why do you stand looking up toward heaven? This Jesus, who has been taken up from you into heaven, will come in the same way as you saw him go into heaven.'

There are many important, crucial, yes, even <u>great events</u> that never get into the newspaper. You don't hear about them on the radio or the TV. For example, helpful, positive events occur in the Hilltop each day but these go almost always unnoticed. In your own life, there are blessings that abound but at times even your family is not aware of these. Much could be shared today that is truly significant for you and me, but is rarely heard. Today, I do want to share a message about three <u>Great Events No One Talks About</u>.

The Great Event of the Ascension of Jesus.

The Great Event of Preaching.

The Great Event of Waiting.

We in this church are still celebrating the Resurrection of Jesus. We have heard for Sundays how the life, death, and resurrection of Jesus have produced salvation for the world and for you and me. But who speaks of the Ascension of Jesus? Is there anyone proclaiming that event we heard in our scripture this morning?

Forty days after Jesus arose from the dead, He ascended into heaven. The disciples were gathered together for this last time with Jesus on the Mount of Olives. For forty days Jesus had shown himself with mighty, convincing appearances to them. As Jesus talked with them, He gave them a blessing. Then He arose into the sky until He was gone from their sight. The early disciples declared that Jesus had returned to heaven – to the Father. They proclaimed that he sits on the right hand of God the Father Almighty.

The Ascension of Jesus is a great event for these reasons:

1. The return to heaven signals the mission and ministry of Jesus has been completed. His work is over. His return is the Father's stamp of approval on what the Son has accomplished.

2. Jesus is now Lord. He sits at the right hand of the Father. He is no longer the so-called 'meek and mild' Jesus – rather He is the powerful One.

3. The third reason the Ascension is so great is that Jesus sends the Holy Spirit upon His disciples after He returns to heaven.

John 16:7 - 'But I am telling you the truth; it is better for you that I go away, because if I do not go, the Helper will not come to you. But if I go away then I will send him to you.'

Luke 24:49 – 'And I (Jesus) myself will send upon you what my Father has promised. But you must wait in the city until the power from above comes down upon you.'

The Ascension is the Great Event that ushers in for God's people – for the church – for you and me – the power of the Holy Spirit.

Jesus in heaven prays for us. What a blessing to have someone – anyone – pray for us. I know Mrs. Selma Muller prays for me – my wife prays for me – but I am astonished that Jesus prays for me. In the great 8th chapter of Romans we read many astonishing promises – 'Christ Jesus, who died, yes, who was raised, who is at the right hand of God, who indeed intercedes for us.' (Romans 8:34) 'Intercedes' means 'to pray for' – Jesus prays now for you. Wow!

Jesus commissions His disciples to go into the world. We are His witnesses. In the power of the Holy Spirit, God's people are to start in Jerusalem and then move out for a world-wide mission.

Jesus promises to return again. The angels tell us not to stand around looking into the sky. The angels declare that Jesus will return again in power and glory to create a new heaven and earth.

The above six reasons are the basis for declaring that the Ascension of Jesus is a great event and even though no one talks about it, you and I can't help but be inspired and empowered. This leads me to my second point, the great event of preaching.

As a whole, our society isn't excited about preaching. There are a few little phrases that we use to point to the disinterest – 'don't preach to me,' we say. Yet, preaching is a great event.

Jesus tells His disciples that everything has been accomplished. Jesus' life has fulfilled scripture. These events are the foundation of a new life for everyone, but someone needs to preach this word of life. Jesus tells of the importance of preaching His message. Jesus proclaims that this message is for the nations. You and I are to be the preachers. All who name the Name of Jesus are His preachers.

<u>Depth study on the Message – the Direction – and the Instrument</u>

The Message – Jesus' life and resurrection as fulfillment of God's plan in Scripture.

- o This message includes a call to repentance – turning around in life – a change of mind – moving to God.

- o This message includes a sharing of forgiveness – our sins are taken away – all is forgiven.

- o This message is also directed to you and me.

- o This message bears results – in a recent couple's retreat I heard this from a man who shared with me – 'I came as an agnostic. I go home as a Christian.'

The Direction

- o All nations, everybody, even people we don't know.

- o People we often write off as not interested.

- o Begin in Jerusalem, that is, at home. Jesus asks the disciples to start where they had failed.

The Instruments – You will be my witnesses (Acts 1:8). We are the preachers. All of us! In Jesus you and I can be effective preachers.

The final great event no one is talking about is that of <u>Waiting on the Lord</u>. Jesus instructed His disciples to wait for the power from on high – to wait for the Holy Spirit.

There is the active side of life in Jesus but there is also the passive side. You work at a job but you wait for spring. You wait for a baby – for God's Word to blossom in a life.

The Book of Psalms in the Bible encourages a disciple to wait <u>on</u> the Lord – wait <u>in</u> the Lord. There is a time for us preachers to wait in faith.

Many of you have now planted a garden. The tiny plants are just beginning to grow. You can do a little weeding but it is really a season of waiting.

Waiting on the Lord says something about patience, relying upon God, and listening for God to speak to you. The disciples had to wait days before the Holy Spirit came.

I can't tell you 'how long' or even 'when' but there are seasons for the preachers to wait in God's Kingdom. Time when you don't know the answer. Time of illness.

Wait on the Lord for God will surely answer you and show you and empower you.

There are great events that no on talks about.

> The Great Event of the Ascension.
>
> The Great Event of Preaching.
>
> The Great Event of Waiting.

These are not considered great by the world's standards, yet for God's people these are great because these are of God and God Is Great!

_5_

PENTECOST IS NOW

The Festival of Pentecost

May 30, 1993

Acts 2:1-21

When the day of Pentecost had come, they were all together in one place. ²And suddenly from heaven there came a sound like the rush of a violent wind, and it filled the entire house where they were sitting. ³Divided tongues, as of fire, appeared among them, and a tongue rested on each of them. ⁴All of them were filled with the Holy Spirit and began to speak in other languages, as the Spirit gave them ability.

⁵ Now there were devout Jews from every nation under heaven living in Jerusalem. ⁶And at this sound the crowd gathered and was bewildered, because each one heard them speaking in the native language of each. ⁷Amazed and astonished, they asked, 'Are not all these who are speaking Galileans? ⁸And how is it that we hear, each of us, in our own native language? ⁹Parthians, Medes, Elamites, and residents of Mesopotamia, Judea and Cappadocia, Pontus and Asia, ¹⁰Phrygia and Pamphylia, Egypt and the parts of Libya belonging to Cyrene, and visitors from Rome, both Jews and proselytes, ¹¹Cretans and Arabs—in our own languages we hear them speaking about God's deeds of power.' ¹²All were amazed and perplexed, saying to one another, 'What does this mean?' ¹³But others sneered and said, 'They are filled with new wine.'

¹⁴ But Peter, standing with the eleven, raised his voice and addressed them, 'Men of Judea and all who live in Jerusalem, let this be known to you, and listen to what I say. ¹⁵Indeed, these are not drunk, as you suppose, for it is only nine o'clock in the morning. ¹⁶No, this is what was spoken through the prophet Joel: ¹⁷"In the last days it will be, God declares, that I will pour out my Spirit upon all flesh, and your sons and your daughters shall prophesy, and your young men shall see visions, and your old men shall dream dreams. ¹⁸Even upon my slaves, both men and women, in those days I will pour out my Spirit; and they shall prophesy. ¹⁹And I will show portents in the heaven above and signs on the earth below, blood, and fire, and smoky mist. ²⁰The sun shall be turned to darkness and the moon to blood, before the coming of the Lord's great and glorious day. ²¹Then everyone who calls on the name of the Lord shall be saved."

I received my first Pentecost card on Thursday. I was very encouraged. I mentioned last Sunday that I didn't receive any Ascension Day cards in the mail and I didn't expect any Pentecost cards, but I was mistaken – which is about average for me.

Life is full of wonderful surprises. Life is especially full of surprises for God's people. We should always be ready for God to surprise us.

Go back to Pentecost two thousand years ago. Pentecost was a festival 50 days after Easter. The disciples are gathered together in Jerusalem. Jesus had directed them to stay together – to remain in Jerusalem and to wait.

We don't know how many were gathered but there were more than the twelve – maybe as many as 120. They were praying. There is this ear-splitting roar of wind. Next came a fire that splits into tongues of 'fire' which is distributed to all – a fiery tongue hovering over each person. This group of believers (mostly uneducated people) begins to speak in a variety of languages to a large assembly of people from Jerusalem. The fire-empowered believers speak of the wonderful acts of God. They speak of the wonderful acts of God!

Are you ready for another miracle? Simon Peter 'stands up' and he 'speaks out.' This one who had betrayed Jesus – denied Jesus three times. This one stood up and interprets the Pentecost event. Simon Peter preaches the good news of Jesus and the result is that 3000 people are baptized and added to God's church – Glory Hallelujah!

My theme is Pentecost Is Now! God's Gift For Mission Unto Salvation is how I want to break down and preach this theme.

God's Gift

God gives many blessings – too many to count. The gift of the Holy Spirit is the special blessing upon which we now focus. The Bible says that all of the disciples – yes all – were filled with the Holy Ghost (Holy Spirit). That is worth pondering – meditating upon.

What is it that we are filled with?

As I walked the streets this week I met at South 23rd and M Street an old friend – Ebony. I have known her since she was a child – a difficult life – now as a teenager – trying to be 'grown up.' She is there on the corner with her drug buddy. She is being treated like a worthless, forsaken dog. She receives a tongue lashing with down-cast head and eyes. Despair is filling her heart and mine.

A little further across the street is a gang of young men. I talk briefly but only Jeffrey really wants to share. We talk. He is confused and frightened for his future.

With what am I filled? Hate? Despair? Lust? Greed?

The great good news today is that God's gift is for you and me. God wants to give you the Holy Spirit. God wants to give a Presence – a Helper – a Truth – a Friend – a Defender – so that your life – my life – Ebony's life – Jeffrey's life – may change for the better.

The Holy Spirit at Pentecost changed the disciples. In what ways? Many. Consider just one. These men and women and children were able now to witness for Jesus. Like Simon Peter, they, too, stood up and shared a witness for Jesus.

God's Gift for Mission

The first believers continued to move out in God's Spirit. God's Holy Spirit is power (dynamite). (Acts 1:8) 'You shall receive power (a good translation for the word power is <u>dynamite</u>) when the Holy Spirit shall come upon you.'

However, beware of being filled with pride. Soren Kierkegaard wrote a parable that describes the conduct of too many Christians. Kierkegaard describes Christians as similar to geese in a barnyard that always gathered every seven days. A leader flies up to the fence post and addresses the flock. He always speaks of the glories of their ascension – how they flew high in the sky. Some of the geese are so worked up that they flapped their wings but <u>no one</u> took off because the corn tasted mighty good and the barnyard was very secure.

God help us to be more – share more – to be in the Spirit.

<u>Pentecost Is Now</u>. Are you trying to be a Christian today? A Christian student? Mom or Dad? Pastor?

We have a great baseball team of young men, 4th – 6th graders. I watch them play each week. They are learning. One of the most difficult lessons is to <u>swing</u> at the baseball – to take a risk. Christianity is meant to be risky – to count on God's Spirit so that we <u>act</u>. As with our baseball team, we are learning in the Spirit to grow – to try.

God's Gift for Mission Unto Salvation

The final verse in our scripture reading is Acts 2:21 – 'And everyone who calls on the name of the Lord will be saved.' Simon Peter shared these words with this large array of people.

The Holy Spirit used Simon Peter's message and the witness of the 120 to the gracious effect that 3000 people were saved that day. Three thousand repented – believed – were baptized. God's salvation came to them and God's salvation through the Holy Spirit comes to us. True, God was not finished with these folk. Growth in the Spirit would be a life-long process. Risk-taking is a daily event, but as the old spiritual bit of wisdom says:

'I am not what I should be.

I am not what I could be.

But thank God, I am not what I used to be.'

Could that happen – could the Pentecost event happen – here in Tacoma – at Peace Lutheran Church?

You betcha!

Am I trying? Am I swinging at the opportunities God sends my way? Are we trying?

God has not given up on Jeffrey – on Ebony – on you and me. God's Spirit will continue to work. Right now. Maybe not as we think but salvation will come.

'Pentecost Is Now!'

'God's Gift for Mission Unto Salvation'

Join me in a prayer for this occasion from our green hymnal*.

God, the Father of our Lord Jesus Christ, as you sent upon the disciples the promised gift of the Holy Spirit, look upon your Church and open our hearts to the power of the Spirit. Kindle in us the fire of your love, and strengthen our lives for service in your kingdom; through you Son, Jesus Christ our

Holle Plaehn

Lord, who lives and reigns with you in the unity of the Holy Spirit, one God, now and forever. Amen.

*Lutheran Book of Worship

_6_

THE RIGHTEOUSNESS OF GOD THROUGH FAITH IN JESUS CHRIST FOR ALL WHO BELIEVE
Reformation Sermon

October 31, 1999

Romans 3:19-28

Now we know that whatever the law says, it speaks to those who are under the law, so that every mouth may be silenced, and the whole world may be held accountable to God. 20For 'no human being will be justified in his sight' by deeds prescribed by the law, for through the law comes the knowledge of sin.

21 But now, irrespective of law, the righteousness of God has been disclosed, and is attested by the law and the prophets, 22the righteousness of God through faith in Jesus Christ - for all who believe. For there is no distinction, 23since all have sinned and fall short of the glory of God; [24]*they are now justified by his grace as a gift, through the redemption that is in Christ Jesus,* [25]*whom God put forward as a sacrifice of atonement - by his blood, effective through faith. He did this to show his righteousness, because in his divine forbearance he had passed over the sins previously committed;* [26]*it was to prove at the present time that he himself is righteous and that he justifies the one who has faith in Jesus.*

Many years ago – far, far away – there was a man who was addicted. His name was Martin Luther and he lived in Germany over 500 years ago.

Now, this man looked pretty good on the outside. He was a priest. He was a college and seminary graduate. He had an earned doctor's degree. Often he worked from dawn to dusk. He preached/taught students and wrote books. He was eloquent and a great debater. Martin Luther would be used by God to make dynamic changes in church and society. But did I mention to you that he was addicted?

You see, Luther did things that were wrong – sinful – and no matter how hard he tried, <u>and he did try</u>, he knew deep down he was addicted. Luther would often call his addiction 'sin' or similar names. So Luther agonized as to how he could stand before the Righteous God. This God who was <u>right</u> – always right in word and deed. How? God was great and pure and holy and Luther realized he was none of those. Yes, Luther was addicted and all of us know at least one more addict – <u>ourselves</u>! We, too, in moments of truth realize our own addiction.

Luther believed that our addiction was basic to our nature – yes and there was in ourselves no hope for recovery.

Well, that was Luther – how about you? Me? 'For all have sinned and fall short of the glory of God.' (Romans 3:23)

> Are you a sinner?
> Are you in need for a Savior?
> Are you an addict?

Addiction and Faith in Jesus the Christ

If you are not addicted, I have nothing to share that will help you. But if you are an addict, please hear of a gracious, freeing name – Jesus the Christ. For in that name and in that person there is good news from God.

I am not proclaiming an idea, I am speaking of a <u>continuing experience</u> that comes as you and I or <u>anyone</u> put faith in Jesus. This Jesus is from the righteous God who loves you. Yes, and the response from you and me is to trust Jesus and receive forgiveness and liberty.

Each day God calls you and me to faith in Jesus. 'The righteousness of God through faith in Jesus Christ for all who believe.'

So I ask again, invite again <u>you</u> to faith in Jesus for cleansing and forgiveness, and to believe in Jesus for a daily experience of grace.

Addiction and Reformation

Finally, I want to focus on addiction and reformation.

For what purpose has God called you and me? There are many reasons but on this day, I believe the call in Jesus is for reformation, that is, assisting in the reformation of our world and in our church.

Reformation means to transform our world to be a more <u>just</u> society and to transform our churches to be communities of faith, fire, and love. Two examples:

> Martin Luther King, Jr. in his efforts to change the world. His dream (God's dream) was justice for all. Remember, too, he was not alone in this endeavor. Thousands of dedicated people marched with him. These, too, made progress in civil rights and justice for all a reality in our land.

> Rosa Lee Parks. She refused to move to the back of the bus. Yes, this dramatic action is well known. What is less known is her entire life of service and witness for peace and justice.

Our world needs reformation. You and I and all believers are an important part of God's answer to renew, to correct, to bring justice to our land. The church always needs to have the Holy Spirit bring fire and zest to God's people. You and I through God's power can be reformers during our time.

'The Righteousness of God through Faith in Jesus Christ for All Who Believe.'

_7_

JOY THROUGH SEEING THE HIDDEN CHRIST
Third Sunday of the Resurrection of Jesus

May 3, 1987

Luke 24:14-35

¹⁴They were talking with each other about all these things that had happened. ¹⁵While they were talking and discussing, Jesus himself came near and went with them, ¹⁶but their eyes were kept from recognizing him. ¹⁷And he said to them, 'What are you discussing with each other while you walk along?' They stood still, looking sad. ¹⁸Then one of them, whose name was Cleopas, answered him, 'Are you the only stranger in Jerusalem who does not know the things that have taken place there in these days?' ¹⁹He asked them, 'What things?' They replied, 'The things about Jesus of Nazareth,⋇ who was a prophet mighty in deed and word before God and all the people, [20]and how our chief priests and leaders handed him over to be condemned to death and crucified him. [21]But we had hoped that he was the one to redeem Israel. Yes, and besides all this, it is now the third day since these things took place. [22]Moreover, some women of our group astounded us. They were at the tomb early this morning, [23]and when they did not find his body there, they came back and told us that they had indeed seen a vision of angels who said that he was alive. [24]Some of those who were with us went to the tomb and found it just as the women had said; but they did not see him.' [25]Then he said to them, 'Oh, how foolish you are, and how slow of heart to believe all that the prophets have declared! [26]Was it not necessary that the Messiah should suffer these things and then enter into his glory?' [27]Then beginning with Moses and all the prophets, he interpreted to them the things about himself in all the scriptures.

[28] As they came near the village to which they were going, he walked ahead as if he were going on. [29]But they urged him strongly, saying, 'Stay with us, because it is almost evening and the day is now nearly over.' So he went in to stay with them. [30]When he was at the table with them, he took bread, blessed and broke it, and gave it to them. [31]Then their eyes were opened, and they recognized him; and he vanished from their sight. [32]They said to each other, 'Were not our hearts burning

within us while he was talking to us on the road, while he was opening the scriptures to us?' [33]*That same hour they got up and returned to Jerusalem; and they found the eleven and their companions gathered together.* [34]*They were saying, 'The Lord has risen indeed, and he has appeared to Simon!'* [35]*Then they told what had happened on the road, and how he had been made known to them in the breaking of the bread.*

Do you hear it?

Do you see it?

No, I don't either, but we know it is there!

If I had a radio here and turned on the radio, we would hear the sound waves that surround us. If I had a TV, we could see those waves that also surround us. We cannot always see or hear what is present. Even so – this day – I ask, do you hear the Risen Christ? Do you see Him?

Not only in this sanctuary, but this Risen Jesus is in our homes – on the streets – in school – in the focus of people who touch our lives. I want to speak to you in this Easter Season of <u>Joy through Seeing the Hidden Christ</u>.

My contention is that the Risen Christ is here and can be seen and can be heard by you and me. There are three parts to this message:

I.   Christ Hidden in the World

II. Christ Hidden in the Word

III. Christ Hidden in the Bread

In the Gospel of St. Luke, we heard today of two disciples. The time is the afternoon of Easter – these disciples are on their way from Jerusalem to a little town called Emmaus. These men have been shattered by the recent death of Jesus. They did not believe in the circulating reports that Jesus had been resurrected. So they walked along in their gloom and doom.

The Bible says that 'they had hoped' that Jesus was the one sent by God, but those were unfounded hopes. At least, so it seemed to them. In this atmosphere of doubt and despair, Jesus comes. Jesus catches up with them, walks with them, talks with them, Jesus reaches out to them. <u>This was true for them and it is true for us</u>!

I cannot speak for the billions of folk on this planet, but I know that God in Christ has reached out to me – many times – many ways – working with me to bring me, keep me, in Jesus.

Yes, at times I am not listening. I may not be seeing Jesus, but He is as real as those sound waves and TV waves that surround you and me today. The issues I raise with myself and with you are

>Am I Listening?
>Am I seeing?
>Am I receptive?

What is it that will get our attention? My contention today is that the Risen Christ is experienced by <u>all of us</u> – that Jesus does come to us. Have I seen and heard?

Are you acquainted with Mother Theresa? She is a Roman Catholic nun who has become famous in her later years of life. She and her other sisters walk the streets of Calcutta, India picking up dying people, taking them to a type of nursing home, and providing tender, loving care for them until they die or recover. She contends that she <u>sees in the eyes of these people the Eyes and the Face of Jesus</u>! The point is that in her experience – yes, also our experience – <u>Jesus appears</u>!

Mother Theresa wrote this: 'Never let anything so fill you with sorrow that you forget the joy of <u>Christ Risen</u>!'

Yes, Christ is hidden, but He is hidden <u>in the world</u> so that I may see him and believe.

However, if you can't see or hear the Risen Christ in the world then may we push on to consider Christ Hidden <u>in the Word</u>. As Jesus walked with those two gloomy disciples, He instructed them in the Word of God – the Bible.

Verse 27 – 'And beginning with Moses and all the prophets, he interpreted to them in all the scriptures the things concerning himself.' Later they said, 'Did not our hearts burn within us while He talked to us on the road, while He opened to us the scriptures.'

The Bible – the Word of God – is all around us - here at church, in our home. We, too, can be instructed so that <u>a fire</u> is set in our lives by the Holy Spirit.

This past week I saw a man who came to the Feeding Program lying on the grass outside the door. He was reading. Later, as he came in the basement, I saw him reading. What was it, I wondered – then I saw. He was reading the Bible!

This same week at a crowded dinner table I saw this beautiful little girl – third or fourth grade – she sat reading the Bible! These examples and the example in Luke encourage me to read the Bible – not because I have to – not as some lucky rabbit's foot – but as one who is <u>receptive to Jesus</u>. Yes, so that Jesus may teach me. Ah, there it is again – the key for you and me is to be <u>receptive</u>.

In a practical manner, consider four suggestions this morning in being receptive to the Word of God.

1. Establish or continue a devotional time each day. Read the Bible and maybe some helpful book like *Christ in our Home*. Begin this process and conclude it in prayer.

2. Take time out to meditate upon some basic concept or idea in God's Word. Think. Pray. Listen. Roll it over in your mind. Listen.

3. Participate in a group Bible study – for example, Sunday School or Home Bible Study. Listen to what God says to others. This also curbs some of our own excesses or blind spots.

4. Listen and then apply what you hear in the Word of God. Action.

Finally, I proclaim to you that Christ is hidden in the Bread. Today, we are celebrating Holy Communion. Consider the Bread on the altar.

In our Bible story today, Luke tells us that Jesus was at the table with those two disciples – 'Jesus took the bread and blessed, and broke it, and gave it to them . . . And their eyes were opened and they recognized him.'

In the mystery of God's love, Holy Communion is a means of God to open our eyes and, yes, to open our ears to hear and see the Risen Christ. This has been the experience of the church throughout the ages. Jesus indeed is the Host. Jesus is hidden but revealed not only in Communion but in the bread at every meal. God is the Provider of the food we share here in the church and in our homes or restaurants or wherever we eat. There is the old saying "Christ is the unseen guest at every meal.'

My theme today is Joy through Seeing the Hidden Christ. I have not mentioned 'joy' specifically in this sermon; however, joy does come. Joy will sooner or later come to any life that 'sees' Jesus. Joy is a gift of God. Joy in this life anticipates the experience we shall have with God in the life to come. Joy is a by-product of Christian faith – not a goal we strive for but an unforeseen blessing that comes like the sunrise. Joy comes as Jesus is heard:

> In the world
> In the Word of God
> In the bread

Note: I mentioned that this sermon was preached May 3, 1987. I noticed in the church bulletin a 'thank you' to all who assisted, prayed for, donated food for our Feeding Program. April 1987 just may have been the first time we provided meals in our church basement on a large scale. The bulletin noted that we served over 2,000 meals in April. That was a good start!

_8_

'LET JUSTICE ROLL DOWN LIKE WATERS'
Ecumenical Worship Service
St. Johns' Baptist Church

January 18, 1988

Amos 5:24

'But let justice roll down like waters,
and righteousness like an ever-flowing stream.'

I remember years ago being in the other sanctuary of St. Johns' before this present building was built. Pastor Robert Davis, a close and dear friend of mine, was called at a moment's notice to be the revival speaker after the appointed speaker was unable to be present. Pastor Davis began by reading John 3:16 – 'God so loved the world that He gave His only begotten Son that whosoever believeth in Him shall not perish but have everlasting life.' Pastor Davis said that I may not be a great preacher/teacher – I may not be prepared – but you have to admit I have a <u>great text</u>!

My friends, I am not a great preacher/teacher or a successful pastor. I am not as prepared as I want to be. But my friends, you have got to admit <u>I have a great text</u>! If nothing else, when you get home tonight – when somebody asks you about the service – you can say 'the preacher had a great text.'

'Let Justice Roll Down Like Waters.'

Say those precious words with me – 'Let Justice Roll Down Like Waters.'

This text is great because it is from the heart of Amos the prophet, this text is great because it was a familiar and oft-used quote of Dr. King, and it is great because it is from the heart of God.

'Let Just Roll Down Like Waters.'

May I add a final word of introduction? I am profoundly grateful to the powers that be that allowed me – a southerner – yes, a white southerner – growing up and knowing first-hand the ugly, brutal chains of discrimination of black people – so that I consider this evening one of the highest honors of my ministry. To be able to be a speaker in commemoration of Dr. King is a profound honor to me that shows once again the great love found in Dr. Martin Luther King, Jr. and the movement he represented.

Please take time this week to read the book of Amos and read in detail the life of Dr. King.

Earned doctor's degree – pastor – leader. Dr. King died in martyrdom at the age of 39 in a shocking death. I quote from Rev. Jesse Jackson, one of his aides at the time:

> 'King fell over a second story floor railing to the concrete. Blood gushed from the right jaw and neck area. His necktie had been ripped off by the blast.'

Jackson also surmised, 'He had just bent over. If he had been standing up, he wouldn't have been hit in the face. When I turned around, I saw policemen coming from everywhere. We didn't need to call the police.'

Dr. King was taken to the hospital, where despite emergency surgery he died at 8:30 p.m.

Langston Hughes once wrote, in a poem entitled *Dreams*:

> 'Hold fast to dreams
> For if dreams die
> Life is a broken-winged bird
> That cannot fly.
>
> Hold fast to dreams
> For when dreams go
> Life is a barren field
> Frozen with snow.'

'Let Justice Roll Down Like Waters.'

We gather tonight to celebrate, to commemorate, the life, contributions, and witness of Dr. Martin Luther King, Jr., but I believe we also gather to review our lives in the light of the dream – his dream – our dream – God's dream!

'Justice' is often rendered in the Bible by the word 'righteousness.' Justice means to be in <u>Shalom</u>, that is, unity and peace, with one another. Justice means 'right actions and fair dealings person to person,' equal rights for all in God's sight. Justice is connected with God for God desires to bring justice to an unjust world. The Bible says that God is the One who brings justice for the poor, the fatherless, and the oppressed.

Long ago, a young man from the south – South Palestine, that is – went north. His name was Amos. He was a shepherd, a common man who cared for sycamore trees but had <u>not</u> a common faith. Amos spoke the Word of the Lord. Amos said that when God speaks to <u>me</u>, I just speak to others!

Amos spoke when Israel was prosperous – at least the ruling class was prosperous – and they believed that God was with them. Amos (for God) spoke differently. Amos condemned Israel. I quote the gist of Amos 2:6-8. 'Oppression of the poor – slavery – greed – good people deceived and sold for gain – the afflicted ignored – sexual immorality – idol worship – the inordinate pursuit of pleasure.' These were the sins of long ago and so it reads like a shopping list of our day.

Amos roared as a lion to Israel to <u>let justice roll down like waters and righteousness like an ever flowing stream</u>.

As we remember Martin Luther King, Jr., that same type of 'justice call' is trumpeted by his life to our world.

As I read anew the life story of Dr. King this week, I was inspired by the loving and strong home in which he was reared. He was born into a pastor's family, raised in Atlanta, Georgia. Although protected by his parents and his church, even Dr. King experienced again and again the harsh whip of prejudice. Little Martin's best two buddies were the sons of a white grocery store owner. Martin heard the message from the white parents – 'You can no longer play with our sons.' Martin's mother – 'Mommy dear' as she was affectionately called – had the sad experience of explaining 'why' he could no longer play with his friends.

Or the time when young Martin went with his father, who in his own right was a well-respected pastor of a church. They went to the shoe store and waited and waited to be served, only to be told that they must go to the back of the store if they wanted to purchase shoes. Dr. Martin Luther King, Sr. took his son by the hand and left the store.

But I must rush on past many such poisonous insults and discriminations for those are but the prelude to the 'water moccasin' and 'rattlesnake' bites of Southern hospitality that came to Dr. King when he served in his first pastorate in Montgomery, Alabama. We rush to December 1, 1956 when Rosa Parks, a heroic seamstress, sat in the front of the bus – refused to move to the back of the bus and was arrested. Dr. King was thrust into the leadership of the bus boycott.

He could have remained quiet. He could have ignored the call for justice. He could have said 'Later - later when I get more experience - later when I raise my family – later!' No, not later, justice calls <u>now</u>.

> Amos said 'now.'
> Jesus said 'now.'
> St. Paul said 'now.'

Martin Luther King heard the call of <u>now</u> and heeded that call. What call do you and I hear?

During the Montgomery Bus Boycott of 1956, Dr. King's home was bombed; he received 30 to 40 death threat telephone calls <u>a day</u>; and a shotgun blast hit their home, shattering their front window. This was the prelude to years of salacious abuse by our government officials, including the F.B.I. He spent countless days in court, days in jail and prison (he went to maximum prison in Georgia for a traffic violation).

Sixty days after he received the Nobel Peace Prize in 1964, he was in a Selma, Alabama jail. Dr. King's reaction to this was a message he always preached – the message he preached from the front porch after his home was bombed:

> "Now let's not become panicky; if you have weapons take them home; if you do not have them, please do not seek to get them. We cannot solve this problem through retaliatory violence. We just meet violence with non-violence. We must remember the words of Jesus: He who lives by the sword will die by the sword. We just love our white brothers.'

Tarry with me a little longer as I apply this to our day – this call to justice – this noble example of God's witness.

Let Justice Roll Down Like Waters!

And what do we see as we look over this land? Do we not still see races divided – here in Tacoma – prejudice – open hostility? Is there justice?

Where is the justice in our land when a few make extraordinary salaries and large numbers of households are below the poverty level? Is there justice in that many of our young people are under-educated? Where is the justice in young men and women – not to mention the old – hanging around our corners with never a meaningful job and no hope for the future?

I am tired of riding my bicycle down the streets of Hilltop and seeing the waste of good young men and women on idleness, drugs and sex. Where is the justice of hunger in our land and the millions who die of hunger throughout the world? Where is the justice in making the devil's weapons – so-called nuclear weapons – and holding us all hostage? You may believe differently, but there is no doubt in my mind that Martin Luther King would be protesting nuclear weapons.

Oh, yes, there is still the agenda of justice so Let Justice Roll Down Like Waters. You know the agenda as well as I do! Embrace the dream.

Listen again to a few excerpts of Dr. King's *I Have a Dream* speech in Washington, D.C.:

'I am happy to join with you today in what will go down in history as the greatest demonstration for freedom in the history of our nation.

Five score years ago a great American in whose symbolic shadow we stand today signed the Emancipation Proclamation. This momentous decree is a great beacon light of hope to millions of Negro slaves who had been seared in the flames of withering injustice. It came as a joyous daybreak to end the long night of their captivity. But 100 years later, the Negro still is not free. One hundred years later the life of the Negro is still badly crippled by the manacles of segregation and the chains of discrimination. One hundred years later the Negro lives on a lonely island of poverty in the midst of a vast ocean of material prosperity. One hundred years later the Negro still languished in the corners of American society and finds himself in exile in his own land. So we've come here today to dramatize a shameful condition.'

o o o o o o o

'We have also come to this hallowed spot to remind American of the fierce urgency of now.'

o o o o o o o

'Now is the time to make justice a reality for all of God's children. It would be fatal for the nation to overlook the urgency of the moment.'

o o o o o o o

'We must forever conduct our struggle on the high plane of dignity and discipline. We just not allow our creative protests to degenerate into physical violence. Again and again we must rise to the majestic heights of meeting physical force with soul force.'

o o o o o o o

'No, no, we are not satisfied, and we will not be satisfied until justice rolls down like waters and righteousness like a mighty stream.'

o o o o o o o

'Continue to work with the faith that unearned suffering is redemptive.'

o o o o o o o

'I say to you today, my friends, though, even though we face the difficulties of today and tomorrow, I still have a dream. It is a dream deeply rooted in the American dream. I have a dream that one day this nation will rise up, live out the true meaning of its creed: "We hold these truths to be self-evident, that all men are created equal."'

o o o o o o o

'I have a dream that my four little children will one day live in a nation where they will not be judged by the color of their skin but by the content of their character. I have a dream.'

o o o o o o o

'I have a dream today . . . I have a dream that one day every valley shall be exalted, every hill and mountain shall be made low. The rough places will be made plain, and the crooked places will be made straight. And the glory of the Lord shall be revealed, and all flesh shall see it together. This is our hope. This is the faith that I go back to the South with. . . With this faith we will be able to work together, to stand up for freedom together, knowing that we will be free one day.

'This will be the day when all of God's children will be able to sing with new meaning, "My country, 'tis of thee, sweet land of liberty, of thee I sing. Land where my fathers died, land of the pilgrim's pride, from every mount side, let freedom ring." And if America is to be a great nation, this must become true. So let freedom ring from the prodigious hilltops of New Hampshire. Let freedom ring from the mighty mountains of New York. Let freedom ring from the heightening Alleghenies of Pennsylvania. Let freedom ring from the snow-capped Rockies of Colorado. Let freedom ring from the curvaceous slopes of California.

'But not only that. Let freedom ring from the Stone Mountain of Georgia. Let freedom ring from Lookout Mountain of Tennessee. Let freedom ring from every hill and molehill of Mississippi, from every mountain side. Let freedom ring . . .

'When we allow freedom to ring – when we let it ring from city and every hamlet, from every state and every city, we will be able to speed up that day when all God's children, black men and white men, Jews and Gentiles, Protestants and Catholics, will be able to join hands and sing in the words of the old Negro spiritual,

"Free at last, Free at last, Great God almighty, We are free at last.'

Yes, and let freedom ring from St. Johns' Baptist Church and Peace Lutheran Church and your church.

Let freedom ring from the Hilltop area of Tacoma.

Let freedom ring!

Let it also ring from Tacoma's County-City Building!

Let it ring from our police department.

Let it ring in the job halls and hiring halls of our community.

Let it ring!

And, oh yes, let it ring down K Street and at the Blue-Bird Tavern and Smily's.

Let it ring. Let it ring. Let it ring.

_9_

GRACE

'Through the Bible' Series Sermon

April 29, 1979

The Book of Jonah

¹ Now the word of the LORD came to Jonah son of Amittai, saying, ²'Go at once to Nineveh, that great city, and cry out against it; for their wickedness has come up before me.' ³But Jonah set out to flee to Tarshish from the presence of the LORD . He went down to Joppa and found a ship going to Tarshish; so he paid his fare and went on board, to go with them to Tarshish, away from the presence of the LORD.

⁴ But the LORD hurled a great wind upon the sea, and such a mighty storm came upon the sea that the ship threatened to break up. ⁵Then the mariners were afraid, and each cried to his god. They threw the cargo that was in the ship into the sea, to lighten it for them. Jonah, meanwhile, had gone down into the hold of the ship and had lain down, and was fast asleep. ⁶The captain came and said to him, 'What are you doing sound asleep? Get up, call on your god! Perhaps the god will spare us a thought so that we do not perish.'

⁷ The sailors said to one another, 'Come, let us cast lots, so that we may know on whose account this calamity has come upon us.' So they cast lots, and the lot fell on Jonah. ⁸Then they said to him, 'Tell us why this calamity has come upon us. What is your occupation? Where do you come from? What is your country? And of what people are you?' ⁹'I am a Hebrew,' he replied. 'I worship the LORD, the God of heaven, who made the sea and the dry land.' ¹⁰Then the men were even more afraid, and said to him, 'What is this that you have done!' For the men knew that he was fleeing from the presence of the LORD, because he had told them so.

¹¹ Then they said to him, 'What shall we do to you, that the sea may quieten down for us?' For the sea was growing more and more tempestuous. ¹²He said to them, 'Pick me up and throw me into the sea; then the sea will quieten down for you; for I know it is because of me that this great storm has come upon you.' ¹³Nevertheless, the men rowed hard to bring the ship back to land, but they could not, for the sea grew more and more stormy against them. ¹⁴Then they cried out to the LORD, 'Please, O LORD, we pray, do not let us perish on account of this man's life. Do not make us guilty of innocent blood; for you, O LORD, have done as it pleased you.' ¹⁵So they picked Jonah up and threw him into the sea; and the sea ceased from its raging. ¹⁶Then the men feared the LORD even more, and they offered a sacrifice to the LORD and made vows.

¹⁷But the LORD provided a large fish to swallow up Jonah; and Jonah was in the belly of the fish for three days and three nights.

² Then Jonah prayed to the LORD his God from the belly of the fish, ²saying, "I called to the LORD out of my distress, and he answered me; out of the belly of Sheol I cried, and you heard my voice. ³You cast me into the deep, into the heart of the seas, and the flood surrounded me; all your waves and your billows passed over me. ⁴Then I said, 'I am driven away from your sight; how shall I look again upon your holy temple?' ⁵The waters closed in over me; the deep surrounded me; weeds were wrapped around my head ⁶at the roots of the mountains. I went down to the land whose bars closed upon me forever; yet you brought up my life from the Pit, O LORD my God. ⁷As my life was ebbing away, I remembered the LORD; and my prayer came to you, into your holy temple. ⁸Those who worship vain

idols forsake their true loyalty. ⁹But I with the voice of thanksgiving will sacrifice to you; what I have vowed I will pay. Deliverance belongs to the LORD!"

¹⁰ *Then the LORD spoke to the fish, and it spewed Jonah out upon the dry land.*

³ *The word of the LORD came to Jonah a second time, saying, ²"Get up, go to Nineveh, that great city, and proclaim to it the message that I tell you." ³So Jonah set out and went to Nineveh, according to the word of the LORD. Now Nineveh was an exceedingly large city, a three days' walk across. ⁴Jonah began to go into the city, going a day's walk. And he cried out, "Forty days more, and Nineveh shall be overthrown!"*

⁵ *And the people of Nineveh believed God; they proclaimed a fast, and everyone, great and small, put on sackcloth. ⁶When the news reached the king of Nineveh, he rose from his throne, removed his robe, covered himself with sackcloth, and sat in ashes. ⁷Then he had a proclamation made in Nineveh: "By the decree of the king and his nobles: No human being or animal, no herd or flock, shall taste anything. They shall not feed, nor shall they drink water. ⁸Human beings and animals shall be covered with sackcloth, and they shall cry mightily to God. All shall turn from their evil ways and from the violence that is in their hands. ⁹Who knows? God may relent and change his*

mind; he may turn from his fierce anger, so that we do not perish." ¹⁰When God saw what they did, how they turned from their evil ways, God changed his mind about the calamity that he had said he would bring upon them; and he did not do it.

⁴ But this was very displeasing to Jonah, and he became angry. ²He prayed to the LORD and said, "O LORD ! Is not this what I said while I was still in my own country? That is why I fled to Tarshish at the beginning; for I knew that you are a gracious God and merciful, slow to anger, and abounding in steadfast love, and ready to relent from punishing. ³And now, O LORD, please take my life from me, for it is better for me to die than to live." ⁴And the LORD said, "Is it right for you to be angry?"

⁵ Then Jonah went out of the city and sat down east of the city, and made a booth for himself there. He sat under it in the shade, waiting to see what would become of the city. ⁶The LORD God appointed a bush, and made it come up over Jonah, to give shade over his head, to save him from his discomfort; so Jonah was very happy about the bush. ⁷But when dawn came up the next day, God appointed a worm that attacked the bush, so that it withered. ⁸When the sun rose, God prepared a sultry east wind, and the sun beat down on the head of Jonah so that he was faint and asked that he might die. He said, "It is better for me to die than to live." ⁹But God said to Jonah, "Is it right for you to be angry about the bush?" And he said, "Yes, angry enough to die." ¹⁰Then the LORD said, "You are concerned about the bush, for which you did not labor and which you did not grow; it came into being in a night and perished in a night. ¹¹And should I not be concerned about Nineveh, that great city, in which there are more than a hundred and twenty thousand persons who do not know their right hand from their left, and also many animals?"

Grace is God's love to you and to me. Grace is the unmerited mercy of God. Grace is forgiveness through Jesus.

Grace, according to St. Paul, is described in Ephesians 2:1-9. I select a few verses but please read this entire section of God's Word.

'You were dead through the trespasses and sins in which you once lived . . . But God, who is rich in mercy, out of the great love with which He loved us, even when we were dead through our trespasses, made us alive together with Christ – by grace you have been saved . . .'

'For by grace you have been saved through faith, and this is not your own doing; it is the gift of God . . .'

Grace – God's grace – is a wonderful reality in this world, yet grace is not always understood or appreciated. In the book of Jonah, 'grace' is key to understanding the message of this book.

I will use the theme <u>Grace</u> today.

Stumbling over Grace.
Blooming in Grace.
Cross-bearing because of Grace.

Stumbling over Grace

The story of Jonah is an excellent example of how people (you and I) can stumble over grace

The story

Jonah is a prophet of God called to preach God's Word to Nineveh, the capital city of the enemies of God's people! Jonah ran away from God's call. Jonah wants the Ninevites destroyed. Jonah's hatred makes his life miserable. Finally, after much grace, which includes the rescue of Jonah from the 'great fish,' Jonah goes to Nineveh, but there is no joy in his life or message. The last straw is when (of all things - his worst fear and hatred) the people of Nineveh repent and God spares them. Grace! Jonah wants to die! Jonah can't stand salvation for his enemies and in a sense Jonah can't stand God's grace!

The church has always had its Jonahs. The Gospel has often had to overcome the barriers of race, sex, color, economic standing, etc. Jonah's problem still confronts the church today. On the positive side, this little book of Jonah underscores for us that <u>God's mercy is for all people</u>.

What are your (my) prejudices? Where are we unwilling to allow God's grace to flow? Non-Christians often don't know or won't accept the grace of God. They want to come to God and God's church on some other basis, on their terms. We all at times want another way than grace; this attitude is our sin.

<u>Blooming in Grace</u>

God's grace can be the source for freedom to bloom where you are planted. God's grace overflows so much that you need not run away like Jonah. Rather, <u>in grace</u> you can serve God where you are. As a father – mother – grandfather – student – whatever your position, you can serve God.

Three examples:

Captain Otis Lunde – head jailer in Madison, Wisconsin. As chaplain, I saw his ministry served with strength and courage. Even the prisoners praised him for fairness and compassion. When I began worship services with Holy Communion at the jail chapel, Captain Lunde knelt at 7 a.m. on Sunday with the first group of prisoners for communion.

Grandma Smith in Houston, Texas. I knew her from the first church I served. She raised her daughter's two children in a tiny home on the waterfront, one of the most notorious crime/violent areas of the city. She worked at a dry-cleaners ironing clothes to support the children and herself.

Mountain flowers. Many of them are small, almost unseen. However, these flowers are beautiful so that King Solomon in all his glory was not arrayed as one of these.

God's grace is the good earth to enable you to bloom where you are planted. God's grace is sufficient. God's power is made perfect in weakness.

Cross-bearing because of Grace

Because of God's grace, Jesus came in the world. Because of grace Jesus lived and served. Because of grace, Jesus was obedient even unto death on the cross.

Jesus is the Good Shepherd who lays down his life for his sheep (John 10:11-18).

God tries to help the Jonahs of the church. The teachings of Jesus are a constant reminder for us to re-examine our view of life. Christ's own example speaks loudly to us. As Christians we follow the example of the one who is greater than Jonah (Matthew 12:41), that is Jesus! Listen to Jesus!

According to Jesus, I am called to lay down my life in order to find life (Mark 8:31-38).

Sacrifice is important to Jesus as exhibited in His Words and Deeds. Yes, the blood of martyrs has become the seedbed of the church. God asks <u>much</u> from you and from me.

The story of Jonah has an open-ended conclusion. Jonah is sitting outside of Nineveh waiting for God to destroy his enemies. Jonah is disgusted and provoked to anger and depression. He is so worked up that he wants to die. God does not give up on Jonah – asking questions and pointing to all the children who live in Nineveh. God even reminds Jonah of the animals in the city. 'Does Jonah really want to destroy the children and animals?' God seems to ask. Then the book ends abruptly. No more information provided for the reader of Jonah.

Was Jonah transformed by God's grace? Was Jonah repentant? We don't know!

Perhaps the more important issue is the way you and I are writing the ending of this story within our life.

Has God's grace so carried us along that we are not reluctant, but are channels of God's grace to all?

_10_

CARING FOR GOD'S CHURCH – PLANTING HOPE

October 18, 1982

Ephesians 2:1-10

You were dead through the trespasses and sins [2]in which you once lived, following the course of this world, following the ruler of the power of the air, the spirit that is now at work among those who are disobedient. [3]All of us once lived among them in the passions of our flesh, following the desires of flesh and senses, and we were by nature children of wrath, like everyone else. [4]But God, who is rich in mercy, out of the great love with which he loved us [5]even when we were dead through our trespasses, made us alive together with Christ—by grace you have been saved— [6]and raised us up with him and seated us with him in the heavenly places in Christ Jesus, [7]so that in the ages to come he might show the immeasurable riches of his grace in kindness towards us in Christ Jesus. ⁸For by grace you have been saved through faith, and this is not your own doing; it is the gift of God— ⁹not the result of works, so that no one may boast. ¹⁰For we are what he has made us, created in Christ Jesus for good works, which God prepared beforehand to be our way of life.

'Planting Hope' – this phrase is from a brochure depicting the work of Lutheran World Relief. 'Planting Hope' is the vision and the ministry of Lutheran World Relief (LWR). This organization ties together Lutheran congregations throughout the world to plant hope in the lives of thousands, yes millions, of needy people throughout our precious globe. Through LWR poor people receive clean water, improved crops, health and medical care, disaster relief, and an improved standard of living. LWR encourages justice for all people, including the governmental activities of the nations.

During the month of October, I have endeavored to share God's Word on how we can 'Care for God's Church.' This vision includes not only Peace Lutheran Church but also a world-wide vision. Ponder with me today a message on Planting Hope. Thing 'big' with me! Allow the Holy Spirit to stimulate a 'can-do' spirit within us to witness and to serve locally and world-wide!

Planting Hope

- o Through faith in Jesus

- o Through good works

The greatest hope of this world that is planted in the hearts and lives of people is faith in Jesus.

Ephesians 2 - St. Paul writes that people are dad in sin and disobedience, yet God's love is so strong – so great – that God has overpowered the forces of sin, death, and the devil through the life, death and resurrection of Jesus. Jesus' life is effectual. Jesus brings life as people like you and me respond with faith to God's love.

Verse eight stresses that salvation is <u>a gift</u> – not earned. You have received many gifts – money, love, children, mate, friends. Gifts are free. The greatest gift is Jesus.

Two examples of great gifts that have touched my life are a $65 check and a bouquet of dandelions. When I served as a chaplain in the Dane County Jail in Madison, Wisconsin, a prisoner had a vision of God's care for him. Later, I baptized him. Two years passed and I received a check for $65 for our summer church youth program. I was very startled – this poor man facing years of prison who had earned money in the prison sent me this check. He was being paid 9¢ an hour for his work in prison. You do the math! To me, the amount computes to thousands of dollars in my working world, and he gave it for needy youth, none of whom he knew!

My second example of hope from God came on a difficult day for me. I was depressed, down – it was Good Friday. I was in the old parish house in my darkened office feeling sorry for myself. There was a faint knock at the door – I opened the door to see a small neighborhood girl, around five years old. She had a bouquet of dandelions. She said nothing – she gave the flowers to me. I still believe that God sent this angel to me to plant hope in my life.

My friends, God loves you. Do you know that in your heart? God continually comes in a variety of ways to plant hope within each of us. The greatest gift of hope is Jesus, for Jesus expresses the great depth of God's love for you.

Ephesians 2:10 – 'For we are what He has made us, created in Christ Jesus for good works, which God prepared beforehand to be our way of life.' St. Paul focuses on God's love. God's love enables faith to be active in love. As a child of the King, we are in Christ called to bring forth deeds of the King in our lives. I call the life of good works a life of purpose – a life for real!

This life of good works is what I want to concentrate upon in the second part of this message. Caring for God's church is important because the church is the body of Christ. God planted hope through faith in Jesus and God plants hope in the world through the good works of evangelism and service.

The good work of evangelism is sharing the good news of God's love in Jesus. There are people who have NO faith in Jesus – many people! Someone needs to carry the message. How about you? God has given you abilities – time – money – brought you to a place where you touch the lives of people who don't know God's love. Surely, God expects me – helps me – wants me – urges me to reach out and touch others with God's love.

Some of us are studying a course entitled <u>Witnesses For Christ</u>. The author contends that 78% of people who come into God's church are friends, family, relatives and neighbors of a church member who invited them. Not through revivals – not through pastors – not through door to door canvassing, but through ordinary people like us.

But do I have the ability and the strength? Another way to shape that question is to ask 'Does God have the ability or the strength to enable you to be a witness?' I think so – I know so!

In Ephesians 1:13, God's Word tells us that the Holy Spirit has been given us. Reflect long on that gift – you have the Holy Spirit in you to give you the ability and the strength to witness for Jesus.

In Ephesians 1:19 and 20, God's Word tells us that the power of God that He used to raise Jesus from the dead is available to us. What a power! That power is in you.

Make a list of persons that you want God to help you witness to in this year – add names as they occur to you. Ask God's Spirit to guide you. In God nothing is impossible. (Luke 1: 37/Philippians 4:13)

The final part of this message is planting hope through the good works of service. I stress cooperation and how this is accomplished through Lutheran World Relief and even at Peace Lutheran Church. There is strength through cooperation. As World War II was almost over, Lutherans in 1945 realized that a monumental task of work to help the needy was clearly before them. The task was world-wide and needed an agency that brought together the gifts and resources of Lutheran Christians around the globe. A key phrase in publicity was 'Faith Active in Love.'

(I am in December 2003, adding a few lines. "Lutheran World Relief works with partners in 50 countries to help people grow food, improve health, strengthen communities, end conflict, build livelihoods, and recover from disaster. More than ninety cents out of every dollar LWR receives supports this work in the field.' This quote is from a LWR recent brochure. Ten percent of the gifts we have given and are giving through our capital campaign at Peace Lutheran Church are shared through LWR. In other words, our hunger money gifts are shared in this cooperative, efficient manner.)

Could you build a water well in India? No, but with others, thousands of wells have been drilled.

Could you build and then re-build a printing press in Namibia to assist fellow Lutherans under the rule of South Africa? (The first press was blown up by South African saboteurs.) No, but together we are doing this.

Could you provide a children's/youth program for 30-50 participants from 9 a.m. – 3 p.m. five days a week for a month – feeding them lunch, exposing them to education experiences – sharing God's love in Bible Study. No, but together we did that good work this past summer because we worked together.

Cooperation – working together is crucial – not just Lutherans, but all Christians. Praise God and thank you when we labor together in God's Kingdom.

Caring for God's church – and we need it now. This is urgent business. This is a priority. There is an urgency to the ministry of God's people in and through the church. God bless you as you/we, with faith in Jesus, follow our gracious Lord.

Caring For God's Church – Planting Hope

o   Through faith in Jesus

o   Through good works.

_11_

'THANKSGIVING'
Celebrating the Repayment of Our Church Loan

July 6, 2003

Mark 6:1-13

He left that place and came to his home town, and his disciples followed him. ²On the sabbath he began to teach in the synagogue, and many who heard him were astounded. They said, 'Where did this man get all this? What is this wisdom that has been given to him? What deeds of power are being done by his hands! ³Is not this the carpenter, the son of Mary and brother of James and Joseph and Judas and Simon, and are not his sisters here with us?' And they took offence at him. ⁴Then Jesus said to them, 'Prophets are not without honour, except in their home town, and among their own kin, and in their own house.' ⁵And he could do no deed of power there, except that he laid his hands on a few sick people and cured them. ⁶And he was amazed at their unbelief.

Then he went about among the villages teaching. ⁷He called the twelve and began to send them out two by two, and gave them authority over the unclean spirits. ⁸He ordered them to take nothing for their journey except a staff; no bread, no bag, no money in their belts; ⁹but to wear sandals and not to put on two tunics. ¹⁰He said to them, 'Wherever you enter a house, stay there until you leave the place. ¹¹If any place will not welcome you and they refuse to hear you, as you leave, shake off the dust that is on your feet as a testimony against them.' ¹²So they went out and proclaimed that all should repent. ¹³They cast out many demons, and anointed with oil many who were sick and cured them.

God has been good to Peace Lutheran Church – to this community of faith in Jesus.

God has been good to the members of Peace, friends of Peace, and to this Hilltop Community through the Peace Community Center! Ponder the blessings we have received through the Community Center. God has blessed us with a beautiful, functional building, with programs that assist people and with a future filled with possibilities.

Today, we celebrate those gifts. We also celebrate that we are in the 'black.' Our loan of $230,000 has been paid. We are debt-free! Yes, we still need money for the programs, the staff, and a few capital needs but it is mighty good to pause, if for only a day, and give thanks to God.

Tomorrow? Well, tomorrow the work continues. We have forty children in the morning arriving for Camp Peace. There will be staff needs and issues. We still search for more volunteers. Programs cost money. There are some water valves that need fixing. Oh well, life goes on and on but TODAY we celebrate.

'When I think of the goodness of Jesus, and what He has done for me, my soul cries out Hallelujah! Praise God for saving me.' (*This Far By Faith*, Hymn 269)

As we gather today, I remember the debt of sin you and I have accumulated. Oh, the joy you and I experience through God's love in Jesus to have my debt – your debt – cancelled. To cancel a debt is not easy. Hard work. Sacrifice. Commitment. All these and more are needed and God has paid the debt for us.

In our Gospel lesson today, the scripture reveals that Jesus was not accepted by His own home-town folk – even folk from His church – maybe even members of His earthly family. Jesus seemed to understand that suffering and rejection are a part of the price paid for walking with God. Jesus sent out His disciples with a warning that they, too, would face rejection/suffering. The disciples needed to count the cost of discipleship. At times, they and we need to count the costs – it can be mighty high. The disciples were to shake off the dust from their feet from towns or situations where rejection arose. Keep going. Move on.

This is a holiday weekend. This weekend we remember the United States of America and its Declaration of Independence. Many of us give thanks for our country. A number of us have been blessed <u>but not all</u>. This is a time to consider anew the call to serve in our country's government. We need folk like you to listen to the call to serve. Running for elected office is not an impossible dream. The price may be high. Criticism. Defeat and more. Nevertheless, reflect upon God's call to serve in the government of our country.

At the same time, Christians can remember that we have no abiding home in this world. We are to be ready to face and to endure suffering when the values of Jesus and our beliefs in God are in conflict with our country, our government, or officials who try to deify our world. This walk as a Christian citizen is hard and complex, but we need to be aware that the cost of discipleship is high.

My final thought is to re-emphasize God's grace on this grand occasion. God is good. Some of us are wearing the color <u>black</u> today to symbolize that we are by God's mercy in the black – that is, in economic terms, debt free! We even, as a congregation, have some dollars in our pockets! God is good. God has been mighty good to Peace Lutheran Church and Peace Community Center. We have not arrived. The struggle continues tomorrow, but today we pause in our journey and say with gusto:

THANK GOD.

THANK YOU.

_12_

THE POWER OF GOD FOR SALVATION
TO EVERYONE WHO HAS FAITH
Final Sunday at Peace Lutheran Church

August 17, 2003

Romans 1:8-17

First, I thank my God through Jesus Christ for all of you, because your faith is proclaimed throughout the world. [9]For God, whom I serve with my spirit by announcing the gospel of his Son, is my witness that without ceasing I remember you always in my prayers, [10]asking that by God's will I may somehow at last succeed in coming to you. [11]For I am longing to see you so that I may share with you some spiritual gift to strengthen you— [12]or rather so that we may be mutually encouraged by each other's faith, both yours and mine. [13]I want you to know, brothers and sisters, that I have often intended to come to you (but thus far have been prevented), in order that I may reap some harvest among you as I have among the rest of the Gentiles. [14]I am a debtor both to Greeks and to barbarians, both to the wise and to the foolish [15]—hence my eagerness to proclaim the gospel to you also who are in Rome.

[16] For I am not ashamed of the gospel; it is the power of God for salvation to everyone who has faith, to the Jew first and also to the Greek. [17]For in it the righteousness of God is revealed through faith for faith; as it is written, 'The one who is righteous will live by faith.'

As I considered a final scripture passage that I wanted to share with you, this passage in Romans 1 came to my mind. I especially want to stress verse 16 – 'For I am not ashamed of the Gospel; it is the power of God for salvation to everyone who has faith.'

The writer, St. Paul, begins with thanksgiving and that is where I want to begin today.

I thank God, I praise God for the Gospel, for the love, for faith, and for hope in and through God. I thank God for sending Jesus, for the Holy Spirit, and for the church.

I want to leave here with 'thanksgiving', with 'praise' of God on my lips. I am not at this moment referring to what other folk might proclaim. I speak now out of my own experience with God. I proclaim that God is good! Good when I was a child – <u>good</u> when I was a teenager – <u>good</u> down through the years. <u>Good</u> as I have spent 32 years here. I thank God. I praise God!

Secondly, I thank God for my family and, in particular, my wife. What a blessing from God!

Carol has been <u>for</u> me. She has always been in my 'corner.' Carol, please stand. I/we thank God for you, Carol and applaud you.

I thank God for my children – Kristin, Andrew, Gretchen, Janna, Micah and Jon. Those six are my treasures, my riches! I want to recognize them, their contributions, service and support of this church. I thank God for them – I ask those present to stand and I applaud them.

I thank God for YOU! Members, friends of Peace, neighborhood friends, and supporters of Peace. What a blessing from God. I refer to everyone present and the many others that you represent. I thank God for you and I applaud you. As I depart today, I promise you that you have been, you are, and you will be in my prayers.

In our scripture in Romans 1, there is a good news (that is what the word <u>Gospel</u> means) – the good news of God's love in Jesus. This Gospel is to be received by faith in Jesus. I want <u>you</u> to consider <u>from me</u> that <u>Glorious Gospel</u>, which is the 'power of God for salvation to everyone who has faith.'

Finally, I want to share again the five gemstones around which I have focused my ministry these thirty two years at Peace Lutheran Church.

Grace – God's unmerited love in Jesus. God's grace is the heart of the good news. God's grace is the basis of our salvation, the shape of the face of Jesus.

Faith – Grace is to be received by you and me through faith. God calls us to trust Jesus – to believe – yes, in spite of sin, death, and the devil. Faith leads us to go forward – to get up in the morning – to do the deed – the walk the talk – to build a Community Center and to provide for programs (numerous and effective).

Friendship – The church is strengthened and outreach is promoted through friendship. A person comes to the church and expects community in Christ – expects friendship. Jesus says, 'I do not call you servants any longer, because the servant does not know what the master is doing; but I have called you friends.' (John 15:15) Friends – so we are and need to be.

Evangelism – Peace Lutheran Church lives in a vibrant neighborhood. New people move in all the time. However, new folk are not automatic members of Peace Lutheran Church. We are always in need of reaching out and touching hands and lives. Evangelism is a call from God for your pastor but it is also a call to all of us. Most of the members of our family, friends, and neighbors will not come to Peace unless they are invited. Evangelism is God's commission to us. Our time of witness is risky, hard, but also a <u>blessing</u>.

The final gemstone is <u>inclusion</u>, the Pentecost experience/ empowerment. Some of the people invited will come to Peace. God draws them so that they are incorporated in Christ's community and empowered. It is wrong to invite and then by word or deed tell them to only sit and listen. No, we are to empower people – all people in God's church are to share their gifts, to lead, and to speak out of their spirit-filled heart.

Well, that is what I have tried to emphasize for thirty-two years. Now it is time to move on and to have a new pastor take up God's torch among you.

I close with a story. I begin the story by declaring 'I can now clearly see the blinking yellow light.'

Many years ago, Carol and I used to run the Sound to Narrows race at Point Defiance Park. I am not much of a runner and the 7.6 mile run seemed beyond my endurance. I always trained hard and long for the race. I was never sure that I <u>could run</u> the entire race. However, there was a place in the race when my assurance was always revived. As I started up the last, long, dreadful hill, I always looked for the blinking yellow street light near the top of the hill. The light was near

95

the finish line. Once I saw the light, I took courage for I then knew I was going to finish the race.

Friends, I have enjoyed the race at Peace Lutheran Church. The race has not been easy but it has been good. <u>You have been very good to me</u>.

I have never been so sure of this race but today I see clearly the yellow blinking light. Thank you for this time together. I pass on the torch to you and to others, to your interim pastor, and to the new pastor who will come. God's peace. Carol and I love you. Thank you.

All proceeds from this book will be dedicated to the Peace Community Center Scholarship Fund in Pastor Holle Plaehn's name.

About The Author

Holle Plaehn was born and raised in Brenham, Texas and graduated from Texas Lutheran University with a double major in English and History. He attended Trinity Lutheran Seminary in Columbus, Ohio and was ordained a Lutheran Minister in June, 1963 following graduation.

He served as pastor of congregations in Houston, Texas and Madison, Wisconsin before accepting a call to Peace Evangelical Lutheran Church in Tacoma, Washington, where he served for the next 32 years.

He married his wife, Carol, a school librarian, in 1959 and they raised six children. Holle and Carol are enjoying their retirement and continue to work for peace and justice and to share the good news of Jesus.

Printed in the United States
32768LVS00002B/7-135

9 781420 818888